T0166338

TROUT STANLEY

A PLAY BY CLAUDIA DEY

With illustrations by Jason Logan

Coach House Books, Toronto

first edition

For production enquiries, please contact Michael Petrasek,
Kensington Literary Representation, kensingtonlit@rogers.com
or 416 979 0187.

Published with the assistance of the Canada Council for the Arts
and the Ontario Arts Council. We also acknowledge the
Government of Ontario through the Ontario Book Publishing
Tax Credit Program and the Government of Canada through the
Book Publishing Industry Development Program.

LIBRARY AND ARCHIVES CANADA CATALOGUING IN PUBLICATION

Dey, Claudia
    Trout Stanley / Claudia Dey ; with illustrations by
Jason Logan. -- 1st ed.

A play.
ISBN 1-55245-162-3

    I. Title.

PS8557.E93T76 2005   C812'.6   C2005-904274-5

for Bear

Trout Stanley premiered at the Ship's Company Theatre in Parrsboro, Nova Scotia, August 2004, with the following cast and crew:

Sugar Ducharme: Ingrid Rae Doucet
Grace Ducharme: Krista Laveck
Trout Stanley: Michael Kash

Directed by Pamela Halstead
Set and costume design: Denyse Karn
Lighting design: Bruce MacLennan
Sound design: Frederick Kennedy
Stage Manager: Lisa M. Cochran
Assistant Stage Manager: Christine Meyers

Subsequently produced at the Factory Theatre in Toronto, Ontario, January 2005, with the following cast and crew:

Sugar Ducharme: Melody Johnson
Grace Ducharme: Michelle Giroux
Trout Stanley: Gord Rand

Directed by Eda Holmes
Assistant Director: Natasha Mytnowych
Set and costume design: Kelly Wolf
Lighting design: Andrea Lundy
Sound design: Rick Sacks
Stage Manager: Tanya Greve
Assistant Stage Manager: Sandy Plunkett

Characters

Sugar Ducharme
Grace Ducharme
Trout Stanley

Parents' imaginations build frameworks out of their own hopes and regrets into which children seldom grow, but instead, contrary as trees, lean sideways out of the architecture blown by a fatal wind their parents never envisaged.

— Elizabeth Smart, *By Grand Central Station*
I Sat Down and Wept

The legend of the traveler appears in every civilization, perpetually assuming new forms, afflictions, powers, and symbols. Through every age he walks in utter solitude toward penance and redemption.

— Evan S. Connell Jr., *Notes from a Bottle*

We move between two darknesses. The two entities who might enlighten us, the baby and the corpse, cannot do so.

— E. M. Forster, *Aspects of the Novel*

I would like to learn, or remember how to live.

— Annie Dillard, *Teaching a Stone to Talk*

Those
Boots fit like
a glove

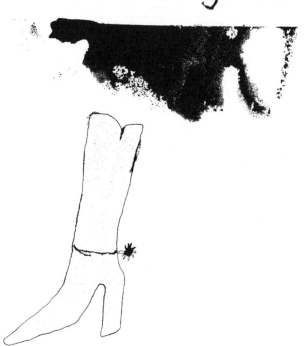

Prologue

Tumbler Ridge, B.C. House beside the town dump. A tidy and trinketful universe. Television, figurines, dinette set. Sugar Ducharme — track suit, crocheted slippers — prepares dinner. Small mutterings, in song form: 'Sugar, sugar, sugar, sugar, sugar, Sugar. Dinner looks so good, it smells so good, it looks so good, you're everything, what, what, what, you're Sugar, sugar, sugar, sugar, Sugar . . .' All finishings finished, Sugar looks out the window. She slinks to the record player. Puts on Heart's 'Magic Man.' She dances — a sultry, buoyant secret. Sound of squealing tires. Needle is pulled, record player turned off. Sugar checks her reflection in the mirror. She straightens her track suit, her slippers, her self.

Enter: Grace Ducharme, through a cloud of dust, coveralls, sunglasses, hair sprayed into a sculpture. Grace and Sugar are twins — they look nothing alike.

SUGAR: You're home.

GRACE: I'm home.

SUGAR: I'm happy.

GRACE: I'm home Sugar, I'm home.

Sugar opens the fridge. Pulls out a soda. She cracks it wide. Hands it to Grace. Grace guzzles.

SUGAR: How was your day?

GRACE: Like the others.

SUGAR: Garbage pickers?

GRACE: No.

SUGAR: Illegal dumpers?

GRACE: No.

SUGAR: Nothin' peculiar?

GRACE: Nothin' peculiar.

SUGAR: I'm happy to see ya Grace. I'm happy you're home.

GRACE: I'm home.

SUGAR: I'm happy.

GRACE: I'm home Sugar, I'm home. *(Grace sniffs the air)* Gonna freshen up.

Grace exits to their bedroom. Sugar is still for a moment, directionless. Sound of freshening up — mostly a keen hair dryer. Timer goes. Ding. Sugar pulls the roast out of the oven and places it on the table. Hair dryer off. To the world entire, Sugar announces:

SUGAR: Roast.

Blackout.

TWIST TIE

STORIES

Act One

Scene One

Midnight. Grace and Sugar are asleep in their bedroom. Front door lock is jimmied open. A man enters. Bare feet. Bearded. Untended and overgrown. A filth to nest in. He closes the door quickly behind him. Eyes adjust. Moves immediately to the kitchen counter, the fridge — finds a half-eaten roast. Eats until he is licking bone. Some growling. Opens cupboard doors until he finds a bottle of something. Tips it back. Swoons a bit. Makes his way to the door. The television. Lured. He sits inches from the screen. Turns it on. Low volume. Switches through channels evangelical: nature, detectives, sports, news. He bangs the side of the television trying to get better reception, remembers where he is, realizes that he has made some noise and dives behind the couch — as Grace Ducharme comes out sleepy-eyed. Grace reaches for the converter to turn off the television, but she is drawn in by the news — as is he.

NEWS: ... Was last seen when she left Rodeo Bob's Steakhouse Emporium and Nude Dancers in Chetwynd, BC, at approximately 3:30 a.m. yesterday morning. Co-workers say she insisted on walking home, refusing rides, despite the nearly torrential rain that night. Not odd behaviour for the independent and some have even said brazen exotic dancer and local Scrabble champion. Authorities have not ruled out foul play, adding that ladies of the night are prone to vanishing. In other news, the caterpillar population continues to —

Grace thinks she hears something. She clicks off the television. Stands still. Scanning. She tiptoes around; the intruder dives and rolls stealthily. She opens the door to their bedroom.

GRACE: Sugar.

Asleep. Starts to close door. Swings it open again.

GRACE: Sugar.

Definitely sleeping. She closes it. Periscoping. Grace decides that there is nothing there. She gets a soda from the fridge, cracks it open and returns to their bedroom. The man comes out from behind the couch. He heads for the door, catches sight of Sugar's crocheted slippers languishing under a night light. He picks them up; he strokes them and sniffs them. Some growling. He puts them back where he found them. Bottle still in hand, he makes his exit.

S PELLS

REGULAR

BROKEN

Scene Two

The next morning. Sugar — track suit, crocheted slippers, humming 'Happy Birthday' — darts about the kitchen making Grace's lunch. She places item after item and packs soda after soda into a large lunch pail. Grace is offstage. Sound of hair dryer — approaching jet engine. Hair dryer stops.

SUGAR: Happy Birthday Grace.

GRACE: Happy Birthday Sugar. Big day.

SUGAR: Big day.

GRACE: Our big day.

SUGAR: Our big day.

GRACE/SUGAR: Lucky thirty.

SUGAR: We had our share o' sufferin' —

GRACE: An' now we're in the clear.

SUGAR: In the clear.

SUGAR/GRACE: Lucky thirty.

Grace enters in a short shorts camouflage zip-up — her hair sprayed into a sculpture. Grace spins for Sugar.

GRACE: Dynamite, eh.

SUGAR: Sure is dynamite.

GRACE: A zip-up. Lates' summer trend. A T-shirt and shorts in one quick zip-up.

SUGAR: Looks hot.

GRACE: Does look hot doesn' it.

SUGAR: Looks hot an' dynamite.

Grace pulls on her cowboy boots.

SUGAR: You got boots too.

GRACE: Like 'em?

SUGAR: Where'd you get the loot?

GRACE: Like 'em?

SUGAR: Where'd you get the loot for the boot?

GRACE: I didn' wan' to tell ya Sugar Cereal, 'cause I didn' want ya to feel left out. But, 'cause ya keep nudgin' me, here it is . . . Ya know the billboard at the Four Corners, the one everybody has to pass comin' in or goin' outta town? Well, it's empty right now an' as you know Stan's Western Gear an' Shootin' Range is no stranger to seizin' opportunity. They were lookin' to do some advertisin' to go along with huntin' season: 'Look out Deer. Look out Moose. We got rifles an' we're lookin' for youse.' You remember that one. Who could forget it? Guess who they asked to be their billboard girl. That's right Sugar. Your very own Graceland.

         Photo shoot was day before yesterday. I wore this very thing. Stood in front of a camo backdrop with a particular glare in my eye. Somethin' between red-hot sexy an' I'm-gonna-squeeze-your-balls-blue dangerous. Irony. That's what we went for. Irony.

         Billboard goes up today. Gonna be a big day in more ways than one. Stan thinks it could cause traffic slowdowns if not accidents. He's hired backup at the store expectin' a crush o' people. That's what he called it: a crush. 'Cause o' me. Graceland, your very own billboard girl. He let me keep the zip-up an' the boots as a token o' his respect.

SUGAR: A billboard Grace.

GRACE: A billboard.

SUGAR: At the Four Corners Grace.

GRACE: Nexus o' the Western world.

SUGAR: You're so lucky.

GRACE: Don' be down Sugar. We get the face we deserve in this life. An' surely you got yours for a reason.

SUGAR: I'm never gonna meet a handsome doctor.

GRACE: Shush it. That is no way to talk.

Sugar serves Grace a hard-boiled egg, Pop-Tarts and a glass of milk.

GRACE: *(breakfasting)* Now you listen to me Sugar. You listen to every word. There is gonna be a plague or a scourge or a flood or some kind o' infestation here. Happens everywhere else. No reason it can't be Tumbler Ridge. Whole country's gonna know about it. Whole country's gonna be glued to their TVs an' radios, callin' in donations, sendin' cans o' soup, sleepin' bags an' hairbrushes. We're gonna be a disaster zone an' when we are those handsome doctors are gonna be comin' in by the busload. An' because we're on the outskirts o' town, we won't be gettin' vaccinated in the gymnasium, in the arena, in the church basement. No Sugar. We won't be gettin' vaccinated there. We'll be gettin' vaccinated right here. Two words, my sweet Sugar Cereal, two words: house call. Knock, knock. An' there they'll be in their white coats with their black bags full o' everything that heals includin' two *(holds up ring finger)* shiny diamonds.

SUGAR: You really think that's gonna happen?

GRACE: I know it's gonna happen.

SUGAR: How?

GRACE: Where's your faith Sugar?

SUGAR: Dunno.

GRACE: Find it.

SUGAR: Can't.

GRACE: Billboard got you down. I knew it would. Darn it. *(back to the boots)* Stylish though, eh. They're the classic cowboy boot. Classic rodeo cut. Fit like a glove. If you came into town, you could get cowboy boots.

SUGAR: I don't want cowboy boots.

GRACE: Classic rodeo-cut cowboy boots. It's what the women who go with the wrestlers wear.

SUGAR: I hate wrestlers.

GRACE: Lates' summer trend.

SUGAR: I don' want 'em.

GRACE: You will if you start mingling.

SUGAR: I hate mingling, an' if I want cowboy boots I'll borrow yours.

GRACE: Who says?

SUGAR: Don' need cowboy boots. Got these *(wretched crocheted slippers)*.

GRACE: Startin' today, you stop wearin' the Holy Mother's clothes.

SUGAR: No Grace.

GRACE: It's done Sugar.

SUGAR: But –

GRACE: It's done, dotted line, it's done. Trust me Sugar. I'm protectin' you.

SUGAR: From what?

GRACE: From her. Every angel is terrible; don' forget that. There's a whole world out there an' you're missin' it. Roads, trees, sun, moon, restaurants, gas stations, bars, boutiques, air. Gift o' the universe. It's time to fill your lungs Sugar. Time to fill your lungs with air.

SUGAR: Makes me faint.

GRACE: Now, this is no way to start our birthday mornin'. It's a fresh decade Sugar, a fresh decade. Lef' your allowance under your pillow.

SUGAR: Thank you Grace.

GRACE: With a birthday bonus.

SUGAR: How much?

GRACE: A toon.

SUGAR: Thank you Grace.

GRACE: One o' these days you're gonna have to spend your money. Instead o' buyin' freedom, you're collectin' dust. You could have new nails, new hair, new teeth, new outfits. I swear sometimes I see mould growin' on your eyes. Now you listen to me. I need to tell you somethin' an' I don' want you to be alarmed. I thought I heard somethin' las' night, more like someone actually. Came out here in my nightie-night an' my hot rollers, moved aroun' like a bloodhound in ballet slippers. Nothin'. But the TV was on.

SUGAR: I didn' turn the TV on.

GRACE: Then who did?

SUGAR: Dunno.

GRACE: Could be a killer on the loose. Comes. Cases us in the midnight hour. No weapons, no men, no problem. Returns in the light o' day when he knows you're here alone, vulnerable as a babe takin' her first breath, not a listenin' ear for miles. He's handsome-ish. Pretends he's lost. He's helpless, lonely, in need. You, bein' one for tragedy an' heartache, let him in to our humble home. Then, after some polite conversation —

SUGAR: He bludgeons me into little steaks. Leavin' me seepin' into the carpet, uncoilin' like a snake, my organs pumpin' in corners, on countertops, one eye rollin' aroun' by the TV stand.

GRACE: A girl's gone missin' Sugar.

SUGAR: No.

GRACE: A stripper. From Chetwynd. She walked home in the torrential rain after her shift, refusin' rides. She was brazen. She was a Scrabble Champ. Now she's —

SUGAR / GRACE: *(Sugar whispers)* Vanished.

SUGAR: We're all jus' lone trees waitin' for lightnin' in this world Grace.

Grace turns on the television.

NEWS: — Our top story: today is her thirtieth birthday, but will she show up to the party? Local authorities are following a trail west towards Tumbler Ridge after an adult paperboy on his morning route found some glitter in the ditch. A teary-eyed Rodeo Bob confirmed that the glitter was indeed part of the Scrabble Champ Stripper's costume — which she was wearing when last seen, now two nights ago … In other news, it's the first day of hunting season —

Grace clicks off the television.

SUGAR: Not again.

GRACE: Today's her birthday.

SUGAR: Her thirtieth birthday. Grace. It's the death spell. We were supposed to be holy, we were supposed to be three, but instead my sister —

GRACE/SUGAR: — it's just you and me.

GRACE: When we los' Ducklin' in the canal, we thought —

SUGAR: — from now on, we're two minutes an' four minutes ahead o' tragedy, but at leas' we're ahead —

GRACE: Not so.

SUGAR: We spent our firs' twenty birthdays in peace —

GRACE: — but like any good storm, the death spell was jus' pickin' up speed before weavin' its destruction. After it took the Holies, it was open season.

SUGAR: Open death season. It's Duckling. It's Duckling an' she's come back from the dead.

GRACE: To punish us for our greed. Our greed for love. Love from the Holies. She hovers above us, an' she won't go away; she's stuck in an in-between world. It's a spell.

SUGAR: An' it's a spell we gotta break.

GRACE: Somethin's fillin' your eyes.

SUGAR: Grief.

GRACE: She's missin'. She's not dead.

SUGAR: She will be. She always is. Every year, every birthday. Nine birthdays, nine bodies. All o' them exactly our age, an' all o' them found by you. Grace, what you have seen over the years.

GRACE: Today will be different.

SUGAR: No it won't. Today will be ten.

GRACE: It can't be.

SUGAR: How do you know?

GRACE: I jus' do. I got a special window into your secrets Sugar. It's okay. We had our share o' sufferin' an' now we're in the clear. Lucky thirty.

SUGAR: Lucky thirty.

GRACE: *(putting on her coveralls)* Gotta go. The garbage is callin'. You don' know what it's like Sugar. Sometimes it jus' takes over. Takes a hold o' ya like a boa constrictor. Ya can't think for yourself. Ya can't speak for yourself. The garbage starts doin' all the talkin', tellin' ya what to do, where to put it. Higher. Neater. Straighter. Cleaner. It's like a room full o' people an' everybody's talkin' all at once an' it gets so loud you jus' wanna scream 'Fire.' Now you bolt up Sugar. You bolt up good. No answerin' the phone. No openin' the door.

SUGAR: Grace you're givin' me the shivers.

GRACE: It's an unpredictable universe.

SUGAR: Everything is vanishing.

GRACE: 'Cept for us. We're here an' we're goin' nowhere.

SUGAR: Is that a good thing?

GRACE: Sugar. Where's your faith?

SUGAR: Dunno.

GRACE: Find it. An' 'member what we said about the Holy Mother's track suit. I expec' a brand new Sugar when I get home.

Grace looks at her reflection in the mirror beside the door, pats her hairdo, puts on her shades.

GRACE: How do I look?

SUGAR: Good.

GRACE: They don' call me the Lion Queen for nothin'. *(She roars. Sugar hands Grace her lunch.)* Sugar. You're my life. Happy birthday.

SUGAR: Happy birthday. *(Grace flies out – a rock-and-roll Mary Tyler.)* Happy deathday.

HAPPY DEATH DAY

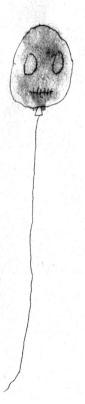

Scene Three

Sugar is on the couch with a large book in her lap. The cover:

SUGAR: 'Smith's Recognizable Patterns of Human Malformation.' *(She opens the book. Shock, horror, compassion. She reads.)* If your child were a bird-headed dwarf, mentally deficient, you could carry him everywhere. The bird-headed dwarfs and all the babies in Smith's manual have souls, and they all can – and do – receive love and give love. If you gave birth to two bird-headed dwarfs, as these children's mother did – a boy and a girl – you could carry them both everywhere, all their lives, in your arms or in a basket, and they would never leave you, not even to go to college. *(sings under her breath)* Bird baby, bird baby, I love you. Bird baby, bird baby, you're so –

She catches her own reflection. She puts down the book. She looks at herself in the mirror – in her dirty track suit. She unzips it slightly and strikes a sexy pose. She is very serious about this. Sultry. The telephone rings. She is startled. Picks it up.

Hello. *(She remembers Grace's instructions, whispers)* Damn it.

Puts the phone down – gently – in its cradle. She looks out the window. Nothing. She goes back to looking at her reflection. Sultry. Reprises Grace. She is struck by a thought. She looks for the phone book, finds it, flips through it, finds a number. She dials.

Hello Stan's Western Gear an' Shootin' Range, I jus' wanted to inquire, comment on your new billboard there at the Four Corners there … Yeah, I was drivin' in from Chetwynd … *(suddenly serious tone)* Oh yeah. Oh yeah, whole town. … Oh yeah, I know. Yeah. … Prob'ly. Mos' likely prob'ly, poor thing. … Does break your heart, doesn' it?

So yeah, the billboard there, wow, it's jus' totally, I'm searchin' for the word here, it's jus' totally, ironic, you know, I

31

mean the girl you chose there, your billboard girl, that look in her eye, it's like, it's like red hot an' blue balls ya know all at once with that camo backdrop, I mean, ironic, totally, yeah, yeah, who is that by the way, who is that billboard girl, it looks to be one o' the Ducharme sisters recognizable from certain tragic events years ago, mus' be a decade by now.

Grace, right, Grace Ducharme. Yeah. *(becoming quiet)* Oh yeah. *(Sugar is silent for a while, listening)* Oh yeah.

She laughs softly.

That is funny … Sure is hard to believe … Yeah … Oh yeah, I guess I, I guess if I was Sugar Ducharme I'd kill myself too.

Oh. Will do. A crush is a crush. Sure was nice talkin' to you too. Thank you Stan, I will pass along your prayers to the good people o' Chetwynd for the Scrabble Champ Stripper, bye now.

She hangs up. She goes to the kitchen. Opens drawers, cupboards. Finds a thick rope. She returns to the centre of the living room. She throws the rope in the air. It swings up and over a rafter, descending like spider silk. Quick. Sure. She is hypnotized by its swing. Back and forth. Back and forth. Sugar fashions an excellent noose. She takes one of the linoleum chairs from the kitchen. She stands on it. She pulls the noose down, placing it firmly around her head. She tugs on the rope to make sure it is secure.

Goodbye Holy Mother. Goodbye Holy Father. Goodbye Duckling. Goodbye Grace. Goodbye Sugar.

Just as she is about to kick the chair away, a man peers in the window. He is handsome-ish, wearing mirrored sunglasses. Sugar screams.

TROUT: Hold up. Hold up pipsqueak. Don't do it. Stay on the chair. Stay on the chair. Steady on the chair.

SUGAR: Why?

TROUT: 'Cause.

SUGAR: What have I got to live for?

TROUT: Mus' be somethin'.

SUGAR: There isn't.

TROUT: How 'bout me?

SUGAR: How 'bout you?

TROUT: Live for me.

SUGAR: I don' even know you.

TROUT: You can still live for me.

SUGAR: No I can't.

TROUT: As a favour. I need help.

SUGAR: We all need help.

TROUT: I'm lost.

SUGAR: We're all lost.

TROUT: I'm desperate.

SUGAR: We're all desperate.

TROUT: I need directions.

SUGAR: Don' have any. Don' know anything. I got nothin' to give. Go away.

TROUT: Take the noose off.

SUGAR: Feels good.

TROUT: Suit yourself.

SUGAR: I am. Stop lookin' at me.

TROUT: Why should I?

SUGAR: I'm cursed.

TROUT: We're all cursed.

Trout turns away.

TROUT: It's a beautiful day.

SUGAR: So? People are dying everywhere.

TROUT: You ever see snails make love?

SUGAR: No.

TROUT: You should. I can't describe it. But you should see it.

SUGAR: I never will ... You called me pipsqueak.

TROUT: I don' know your name.

SUGAR: An' you won't. Ever.

TROUT: Come on pipsqueak.

SUGAR: Don' call me that.

TROUT: Pipsqueak.

SUGAR: Don' call me that. Bugs me.

TROUT: What's your name?

SUGAR: Why do you care?

TROUT: I wanna see how it feels in my mouth.

SUGAR: I'm not tellin'.

TROUT: Look pipsqueak –

SUGAR: Don't.

TROUT: I jus' stumbled into town an' got lost.

SUGAR: *(under her breath)* Oh my –

TROUT: Let me in.

SUGAR: No.

TROUT: Why?

SUGAR: 'Cause I'm no Goldilocks.

TROUT: Listen –

SUGAR: No you listen mister. We're savages, freaks o' the under-
brush. Obviously you're not from around here. Haven' heard
about us. My sister has a bird baby; it's cryin' right now. *(crying)*
Down, Devil, down – that's our bear. *(growling)* He's actin' up.
He'll tear ya apart. The bird baby's screechin'. My sister's angry.
I wanna die. You better go.

35

TROUT: You don' wanna die.

SUGAR: How do you know?

TROUT: You want somethin'. But it's not death. So come on now, there's nothin' 'round here 'cept the Dump an' this place.

SUGAR: No.

TROUT: Why?

SUGAR: There's a killer on the loose.

TROUT: What?

SUGAR: There's a killer on the loose. Girl's gone missin'. A Scrabble Champ Stripper from Chetwynd. She walked home in the torrential rain two nights ago after her shift at Rodeo Bob's Steakhouse Emporium and Nude Dancers, refusin' rides. She was brazen; now she's vanished.

TROUT: You're givin' me the —

SUGAR/TROUT: — shivers.

SUGAR: I know. It's —

SUGAR/TROUT: — heart-stoppin'.

SUGAR: Exactly ... Are you the killer?

TROUT: No.

SUGAR: If you were the killer, would you tell me?

TROUT: Probably not.

SUGAR: Move on.

TROUT: Please.

SUGAR: I can't open the door. I've been left instructions.

TROUT: From who?

SUGAR: My husband. He's a doctor.

TROUT: Oh.

SUGAR: He's very handsome.

TROUT: Lucky you.

SUGAR: Yeah. Lucky me.

TROUT: I've been walkin' for days, for months.

SUGAR: What for?

TROUT: Goin' north.

SUGAR: North.

TROUT: North.

SUGAR: Why?

TROUT: Lookin' for somethin' I lost.

SUGAR: What, your sock, your pen, your homework assignment? *(laughing)* … Are you cryin'?

TROUT: Yeah. I'm fuckin' cryin'.

SUGAR: Watch your froggin' language – this is a Holy zone.

TROUT: Sorry.

SUGAR: Don't apologize. Sorry is an invitation. Sorry is a weakness. Sorry is a disease.

TROUT: Why're you so tough?

SUGAR: You should meet my sister. She's way tougher. Grace. She's my twin. It's our birthday. We were supposed to be triplets but my third sister died in the birth canal. Grace and I called her Duckling like Ugly Duckling because we didn' want to have to compete with her for love from the Holies – the Holies, that's what we call our folks. They're dead. Ten years ago. To the day. Grace. She's prettier than me. She's in the catalogues for local boutiques. An' she's the billboard girl at the Four Corners. You prob'ly saw her when you came into town. She likes to mingle and dress up. The boys love her. They call her the Lion Queen 'cause of her hair. I'm not pretty. I'm scared o' the supermarket. Makes me faint. One question, that's all it takes. Head down, mannin' the cart, checkin' for SuperSaver specials. Then it comes like a blow: 'How's your sister Grace?' An' I'm down. Ears ring, face blows up, eyes go glassy, blackness. Then I hear the hum o' those lights in big fluorescent strips, an' then: 'Ma'am, ma'am, you all right ma'am, you all right?' An' it's like the puberty choir. All these acne-covered boy scouts in their bloody butcher uniforms standin' above me. Crowd gathers an' I can read the tape in their heads: 'She's pregnant, she's sick, she's psycho.' One question, one question, that's all it takes. I haven' lef' the house in ten years. Am I missin' anything?

TROUT: Depends.

SUGAR: On what?

TROUT: Your attitude. See, there's two kinds o' people: the contented and the discontented. The contented stuff themselves with the scenery like a bunch o' wild turkeys criss-crossin' the world grinnin' at strangers. With their photo albums, their spoon collections an' their theme parties, the contented would say you're missin' somethin'. But the discontented — I would fall into this camp, an' judgin' by how I found you this mornin', I would guess that you are also a daughter of the discontented. For us, we're always seein' everything. All too clearly. No matter where we are. Even if it's sittin' on a sofa starin' at a wall, it's still life, an' we know to never take our eyes off it. We miss nothin'.

Sugar takes the noose off.

SUGAR: You can turn around now.

He does.

TROUT: Happy birthday.

SUGAR: Thanks. Lucky thirty.

TROUT: What's your name?

SUGAR: What's yours?

TROUT: Trout.

SUGAR: What kind o' name is Trout?

TROUT: It's a fish name.

SUGAR: Yeah I got that, but why'd your parents name ya after a fish?

TROUT: They died before I could ask 'em.

SUGAR: How'd they die, Trout?

TROUT: Drowned.

SUGAR: Where?

TROUT: A lake.

SUGAR: A lake up north. That's what you lost. Your parents.

TROUT: Yeah.

He starts crying.

SUGAR: Yeah, that is so sad Trout. That's a tragedy. Trout.

TROUT: Yeah.

SUGAR: We're both orphans.

TROUT: Neato.

SUGAR: Trout.

TROUT: Yeah.

SUGAR: You're not goin' to find your parents if they drowned.

He cries more.

TROUT: I still wanna go.

SUGAR: To see it.

TROUT: Yeah, to see it.

SUGAR: To see the death place. I understand.

TROUT: I need your help.

SUGAR: I don' know yet.

TROUT: Please.

SUGAR: Why should I believe you?

TROUT: I never lie.

SUGAR: That's impossible.

TROUT: It's true.

SUGAR: Trout?

TROUT: Yeah.

SUGAR: I don' have a husband. An' he's not a doctor. Or handsome. We don' really have a domesticated bear named Devil for a pet. An' my sister doesn' really have a bird baby. If she did have a bird baby, she'd secretly kill it 'cause it would be too ugly for her to love.

TROUT: You wouldn't.

SUGAR: No. I wouldn' kill my bird baby. I'd love my bird baby. An' Trout?

TROUT: Yeah.

SUGAR: Before, you were wrong, I did wanna die. But now I don't.

TROUT: You're gonna help me.

SUGAR: Don' know yet.

Sugar walks to the mirror, whispering to herself, adjusting her hair, her track suit.

SUGAR: Gotta start thinkin' less about the bird babies an' more about yourself. What's your purpose Sugar? What's yours?

TROUT: You still there?

SUGAR: Sugar.

TROUT: What?

SUGAR: Sugar. My name is Sugar Ducharme.

TROUT: Sugar ... Sugar Ducharme ...

Sugar looks back at her trinketful universe. She takes a deep breath. She unlocks the door. She opens it. Trout in a worn-out cop uniform, carrying a toilet kit.

TROUT: I'm Trout Stanley. How are ya?

Sugar faints. Trout catches her. He lifts her — with tenderness — and places her gently on the couch.

HERE'S

THE GREYNESS

YOU SAW

JUST BEFORE YOU

BLACKED OUT

Scene Four

*Sugar is passed out on the couch. Trout surveys his surroundings. He looks at
Sugar. He touches her feet, sniffs them, starts to sniff the length of her body — up
and down. Some growling. Sugar stirs awake with a belle sigh. Trout wets a face-
cloth, slides in just as she becomes conscious, puts the cloth on her head.*

TROUT: Sh ... sh ... sh. There ya go now, there ya go, easy does it
Sugar, easy does it.

She sits up. Stars in her eyes.

SUGAR: I'm a fainter.

TROUT: I see that.

SUGAR: I'm a fainter o' the firs' degree Trout. But it's not the grue-
some things that make me faint. the gross-out stuff. It's the
regular everyday stuff that puts me down like a dead dog. I
could watch a guy get his arms severed, his stumps spoutin'
blood while a woman's gettin' speared beside me, her kids
kibble on the ground. I could be punctured by a thousand
needles, skin like a bed o' nails while ridin' on a bus where
everyone has food poisoning. I could watch a pileup, a house
fire, a rock concert, an assassination. No problem. But ask me
how I'm doin' — blackout. Grace thinks I need to leave the
house more, more social conditioning. Mingling and such.
Small talk. But I don' see how small talk is important an' I try
to tell her: I don' need it. I don' need small talk. It's space junk,
fleetin' thoughts, fakery. But she's pretty an' wears classic-cut
rodeo-style cowboy boots like the girls who go with the
wrestlers. She's jus' in another world. Will you get me a glass o'
piss water Trout?

TROUT: Course.

While he finds a glass, turns the tap, pours . . .

SUGAR: Grace calls it pill-water-blood-water-piss-water 'cause everyone's pissin' their meds into the lake. All the blue-hairs, the loggers an' the teenage girls. Fish're comin' up man/woman Trout – hermaphrodites with thin blood. But I like pill-water-blood-water-piss-water – I think it tastes good.

He gives her the water.

SUGAR: Thank you. *(tiny sips)* Delicious. Nice to have ya around. I'm usually the one who gets the drinks – 'cept soda, Grace loves her soda, I hate it, soda. I hate it in my core. I do the cookin' too. Crowd pleasers, family favourites, mostly roasts. I'm the wife.

TROUT: Grace is the husband.

SUGAR: In a manner o' speakin'. See really, we're both never-before-married virgins . . . I used to work from home. My own business. A home business. Figurines. It's pretty competitive but I had a certain cachet. I made tragic figurines. Sugar Ducharme and Associates. Specializing in figurines and other homemade items. Specialty items. Tragic items. Upon request, ya know. Got some commissions. Had some momentum. A couple o' the boutiques in town bought my stuff: commemorative figurines o' people they'd lost. The gas station too. An' Madame Button Mushroom Avril, but everyone knows she's crazy. Cancer o' the mind. I stopped makin' things when the Holies died. Los' my will. Now I jus' sit here. But it's amazing how busy I feel. Sandwich?

TROUT: No thank you.

SUGAR: Aren't ya starved?

TROUT: Los' my appetite.

SUGAR: That happens to me sometimes. Once I went on a hunger
strike. That's why I'm way smaller than Grace.

TROUT: Why'd you go on a hunger strike?

SUGAR: 'Cause people shoot squirrels for fun an' I think that's
wrong an' they say, 'Who cares about the squirrels, they're jus'
like rats,' but what's wrong with rats?

TROUT: How long did ya last?

SUGAR: Forty days. Long as Jesus in the desert, but I was a
teenager. It was a real headliner. Had to go to the hospital. Get
tubes put in me, you know, rehydrate.

TROUT: Did people stop shootin' squirrels?

SUGAR: No. Lef' one on my doorstep jus' to rub it in. After that,
people — mostly the squirrel shooters — they started sayin' I was
peculiar. A peculiar kind o' girl. It's tough bein' peculiar in high
school. Grace, she's not peculiar at all. She's friends with the
squirrel shooters; they watch action videos together, think
violent thoughts, drink soda an' eat wings. She doesn't shoot
squirrels herself; she jus' watches. But even that ... An' when
she comes home an' I know she's been there with the squirrel
shooters — I can smell it on her outfit, gunpowder and hickory
sauce — I hiss at her *(hisses)* *sssavage*. Doesn' even make her feel
bad. Still, I got invited to the prom ... as a joke. By Tommy 'the
Joystick' Larue. I hate him. I hate Tommy 'the Joystick.' I hate
him in my core. More than soda. *(imitates Tommy 'the Joystick')*
'Twins twins, What a joke, Mama Ducharme got a poke, Not
from one, but from two, Sugar, Sugar, How 'bout you?' I'd rip
out his eyes if I could but I don' wanna leave the house. Guess

I'm talkin' a lot, bit of a chatterbox — we haven't had a visitor since the double wake.

TROUT: Your parents.

SUGAR: Yeah.

TROUT: Ten years ago.

SUGAR: To the day. It was a real headliner.

TROUT: What happened Sugar?

SUGAR: Don' wanna talk about it.

TROUT: You can tell me anything.

SUGAR: Not this. Blackes' night o' my life; it's a bone in my throat. We're all jus' lone trees waitin' for lightnin' in this world Trout … How do I know you're not goin' to kill me?

TROUT: Ya jus' do.

SUGAR: No I don't.

TROUT: No secrets here.

SUGAR: Why no secrets? I love secrets. I have a million.

TROUT: I have none.

SUGAR: I don't believe you.

TROUT: I never lie.

SUGAR: That's impossible.

TROUT: It's true.

SUGAR: No one never lies.

TROUT: Except me.

SUGAR: Did you sniff me when I was on the sofa?

TROUT: Yes.

SUGAR: Are you on the run?

TROUT: No.

SUGAR: Is that a cop uniform?

TROUT: Yes.

SUGAR: Are you the Scrabble Champ Stripper killer?

TROUT: No.

SUGAR: Would you tell me if you were?

TROUT: No.

SUGAR: You wouldn' tell me if you were the killer?

TROUT: No.

SUGAR: Thought you said you never lie.

TROUT: I don't.

SUGAR: But if you were the killer, you would?

TROUT: I would lie, mos' likely, I would lie.

SUGAR: So you'd be a liar an' a killer?

TROUT: I would.

SUGAR: Gig's up. Get lost.

TROUT: I am lost.

SUGAR: Then get out.

TROUT: Sugar. Don't.

SUGAR: Why?

TROUT: We're jus' beginning.

SUGAR: Beginning what?

TROUT: Living.

SUGAR: That's what the bird babies thought.

TROUT: What do you mean?

SUGAR: Until they met the rest o' humankind.

TROUT: But what if they had a twin?

SUGAR: What if?

TROUT: Would sure make life a whole lot easier.

SUGAR: Are you seducin' me?

TROUT: Secret.

SUGAR: Now, lemme get this straight – you're walkin' due north?

TROUT: Due north.

SUGAR: Some kind o' pilgrimage.

TROUT: Yeah.

SUGAR: To your parents' death place.

TROUT: Yeah.

SUGAR: Which is – ?

TROUT: A lake.

SUGAR: A lake up north?

TROUT: Diamond Lake. My parents were prospectors. Lookin' for precious metals and minerals. That's when the canoe went down.

SUGAR: They had metal detectors on the lake.

TROUT: They electrocuted themselves.

SUGAR: They electrocuted themselves with metal detectors on the lake.

TROUT: They were just startin' out.

SUGAR: Didn' know any better.

TROUT: Didn' know any better.

SUGAR: Must've been a headliner.

TROUT: I wouldn' know. I wasn' there.

SUGAR: How long you been walkin'?

TROUT: A long time.

SUGAR: Months.

TROUT: Years. I'm tired.

SUGAR: So tired o' walkin'.

TROUT: That's right.

SUGAR: Sure is ... Tell me about the snails.

TROUT: What snails?

SUGAR: The makin' love snails.

TROUT: You gotta see it. I can't describe it.

SUGAR: Try.

TROUT: It's slow. Gentle. Wet. Like if mud could make love to
itself. Under water. Over the course o' centuries. Even eternity.
Like all o' the mud's shiftin' is really lovemakin', all o' that rest-
lessness, that undulatin' –

SUGAR: Sounds good.

TROUT: *(continues)* — is really a tongue on your skin turnin' you into openness, turnin' you into light. An' then the makin'-love mud takes the shape o' two tectonic plates that after hundreds o' years o' shy but determined inchin' towards each other — knowin' the other tectonic plate is the only thing you have ever wanted, that hard piece of earth is what you've been missin' all along, is what will complete you now — the makin'-love-mud tectonic plates finally hit, bendin' back, archin' towards the sun, every galaxy starin' down at this calamitous moment, this molten-core moment; this fire throbbin' in the centre o' the planet, peelin' itself from white to red to the muscular wings of a million birds beatin' fast, rhythmic against the air, pickin' up pollen, pickin' up dust, pickin' up entire continents.

SUGAR: Sounds good.

TROUT: Until you are two lost but happy astronauts hangin' from the farthest edges o' what you've ever known. Do you believe in love at firs' sight?

SUGAR: Dunno. I've never been in love. Why? You love me ... My sister, Grace, the Lion Queen, she thinks there's a whole world out there an' I'm missin' it. Roads, trees, sun, moon, restaurants, gas stations, bars, boutiques, air. Gift o' the universe. She thinks it's time for me to fill my lungs. Time to fill my lungs with air. 'Cause that's what humans do. They fill their lungs 'cause they're here to serve a purpose. Whispered to you by an angel into your little unborn ears when you're still in the womb. You know what this is? *(She touches his face.)* This is where the angel puts her mighty glowin' finger after she's told you what your purpose is. Shhh, she says, shhhh ...

Grace'll go to pieces if she sees ya here. She'll kill you an' then she'll kill me an' that jus' won't do.

TROUT: Maybe you're livin' too much for Grace and too little for Sugar.

SUGAR: Story o' my life Trout. Do you want to kiss me?

TROUT: Yes. Have you ever been kissed?

SUGAR: No. Did your parents love you?

TROUT: I don't think so. Did yours?

SUGAR: Too much. Do you like my track suit?

TROUT: No.

SUGAR: It's my dead mother's. I've been wearin' it for ten years.

She starts unzipping her track suit. She stops.

SUGAR: Truth.

TROUT: Truth.

SUGAR: I think I got so much love to give, it's a bomb waitin' to go off.

TROUT: Truth.

SUGAR: Truth.

TROUT: I've slept with a lot of women.

SUGAR: There we go.

TROUT: A lot.

SUGAR: Now we're gettin' somewhere.

TROUT: A lot.

SUGAR: Excellent.

TROUT: An' I have a foot fetish.

SUGAR: That's okay.

TROUT: An' a slight drinkin' problem.

SUGAR: That's okay too.

TROUT: An' I believe in kissing. For weeks at a time. I believe in the uncharted territories of the human brain an' I am against the monarchy. I believe that comin' of age is man's cruellest invention. I believe that forgiveness is overrated. I believe in time travel an' space travel. I believe that cooking is an act of love. I believe in revenge as much as I believe in peace. I believe that the divine is where solitude and togetherness meet in perfect seamless harmonious union. I believe in undying loyalty. I believe that war is a godly trick forcing us to look into the weakest parts of bein' human. An' I believe that our great tragedy is that we haven't thought to look. I believe that the nipple, the tongue, the lips, the place where the ear meets the neck, our eyelashes, as well as our sensual parts, are nature's most gracious offerings. I believe in fragility, slowness an' the long way around. I believe that the soul has a taste, a colour an' a smell, an' I believe that the soul can have orgasms. I believe that we're all animals, an' that anything worth anything comes from the beast within.

SUGAR: The beast within.

TROUT: The beast within. An' I believe that if the body goes too long without touch it starts to wither an' ache. An' I believe that —

TROUT/SUGAR: — no one should ever be alone.

Furious love. Sugar stops.

SUGAR: Truth.

TROUT: Truth.

SUGAR: Stan at Stan's Western Gear an' Shootin' Range said that if he was me he'd kill himself.

TROUT: I'm gonna kill Stan.

SUGAR: Are you jokin'?

TROUT: No, I'm not.

Furious love.

SUGAR: Truth.

TROUT: Truth.

SUGAR: Would Stan be your first murder?

TROUT: No, he would not.

Furious love.

SUGAR: Are you the Scrabble Champ Stripper killer?

TROUT: No.

SUGAR: You love me.

TROUT: With everything in my being.

SUGAR: I didn' really faint. I never do. I jus' wanted to see if you'd
        catch me.

TROUT: An' I did.

SUGAR: You did. You're the first.

TROUT: I'm the first.

*Love. Lamps knocked over. Hydro dams burst, the equinox comes early, parades
everywhere.*

A TWIN REFLECTS

Scene Five

*Sugar and Trout are sugaring and trouting. Front door flies open. Grace —
completely dishevelled, sculpted hair hanging down, coveralls covered in dirt,
makeup streaked from the summer heat. She enters carrying a shotgun loosely
wrapped in tissue paper with a large pink bow on it.*

GRACE: *(closing the door)* Sugar.

SUGAR: Grace.

GRACE: Sugar.

SUGAR: Grace.

GRACE: Sugar, Sugar Cereal.

SUGAR: Grace, Graceland.

GRACE: *(sees Trout)* What the frog, who is this fish?

SUGAR: Trout.

GRACE: What?

TROUT: Trout.

GRACE: What?

TROUT: Trout Stanley. I'm Trout Stanley.

GRACE: Trout Stanley.

TROUT: Trout Stanley.

GRACE: Trout Stanley.

TROUT: Trout Stanley. How are ya?

GRACE: Dunno.

TROUT: You mus' be Grace.

GRACE: Las' time I checked.

TROUT: Happy Birthday.

GRACE: Thank you. Trout Stanley.

TROUT: Trout Stanley.

GRACE: What kinda name is Trout Stanley?

TROUT: It's a fish name.

GRACE: Yeah I got that, but why'd your parents name you after a fish?

TROUT: They died before I could ask 'em.

GRACE: How?

TROUT: Drowned.

GRACE: Great. A froggin' tragedy.

SUGAR: We're all orphans.

GRACE: Sugar.

SUGAR: Yeah.

GRACE: Sugar.

SUGAR: Yeah.

GRACE: *(back to Trout)* Are you on the run?

TROUT: No.

GRACE: Is that a cop uniform?

TROUT: Yes.

GRACE: Are you the Scrabble Champ Stripper killer?

TROUT: No.

GRACE: Why should I believe you?

TROUT: I never lie.

GRACE: Everybody lies.

TROUT: I don't.

SUGAR: It's true.

GRACE: What the frog are you doin' to Sugar – ?

SUGAR: He's showin' me the way o' the snail.

GRACE: Sugar.

SUGAR: Yeah.

GRACE: Sugar.

SUGAR: Yeah.

GRACE: What did I tell ya this mornin' when I lef' the house?

SUGAR: Bolt up. Bolt up good.

GRACE: Why?

SUGAR: Could be a killer on the loose. Handsome-ish, lost, lonely, in need.

GRACE: No answerin' the phone.

SUGAR: No openin' the door.

GRACE: So what the frog – ?

SUGAR: You wanted a brand-new Sugar.

GRACE: I did.

SUGAR: Fresh decade.

GRACE: Fresh decade.

SUGAR: So here I am.

GRACE: Ya look the same to me.

SUGAR: I'm not. Look hard Grace.

GRACE: I'm lookin'.

SUGAR: I'm in love. I'm in love with Trout Stanley.

GRACE: No you're not.

SUGAR: Yes. I am. An' I'm goin' with him Grace. I'm goin' with him to see the world jus' as you dared me to do. Tomorrow. Firs' thing. After breakfast. North. It's done. Dotted line. It's done.

THIRTY
LUCKY

the Eye

its GONE

the

HOLY

MOTHER

Am

3 girls — SUGAR ⎤ TWINS
GRACE ⎦
UNNAMED
(FLEW AWAY)

HOLY FATHER

NOW LONG GONE

TRAGEDY

OTHER STUFF

the Double Birth

THE DOUBLE WEDDING

FAITH — LOVE — DIAMONDS — THE INFESTATION — THE DOCTORS

Scene Six

Trout sits at the dining room table. Grace and Sugar — almost out of earshot — huddle by the mirror. Grace resculpts her hair, her face, drops her coveralls, adjusts her camo zip-up; Sugar watches intently. They put on their party hats.

GRACE: You love me.

SUGAR: Yeah but —

GRACE: That's what love is. Somethin' that grows over time.

SUGAR: Not this kind o' love Grace. This kind o' love hits ya right here *(hits her heart)*.

GRACE: That's make-believe.

SUGAR: Hits ya like lightnin'.

GRACE: That's bad weather.

SUGAR: You can't disagree with me.

GRACE: Sure I can.

SUGAR: No you can't.

GRACE: Why not?

SUGAR: This is the one thing that I know an' you don't … Please, for me. For my birthday present.

GRACE: I already got you a present.

SUGAR: I don't want the shotgun. I want Trout Stanley.

Grace pauses. She spins around. Back to Sugar.

GRACE: Where's my birthday present?

SUGAR: It's a surprise. For later.

GRACE: We were supposed to fall in love at the same time.

SUGAR: I know. But we didn'.

GRACE: What about the double weddin'? We made a promise.

SUGAR: We did.

GRACE: A pact. We're supposed to have —

SUGAR: We will. Done.

GRACE: Dotted.

SUGAR: Done. We jus' need to find ya a handsome doctor.

GRACE: You really think that's gonna happen?

SUGAR: I know it's gonna happen.

GRACE: How?

SUGAR: Where's your faith Grace?

GRACE: Dunno.

SUGAR: Find it.

GRACE: Can't. Don't leave.

SUGAR: I have to. What happened today? You came home lookin' like a buffet in a tornado. You came home early. You never come home early. What happened Grace? You can tell me anything.

GRACE: Not this. You don' know what it's like; sometimes the garbage does all the talkin', bullies ya around. Higher. Neater. Straighter. Cleaner.
　　　Sugar.

SUGAR: What?

Grace pauses, looking at her sister, and then, perfectly resculpted, she spins around, hoists the shotgun and points it at Trout.

SUGAR: Grace. No Graceland.

TROUT: Jesus.

GRACE: There's a killer on the loose.

SUGAR: She's missin' –

GRACE: Shush it –

SUGAR: She's not dead –

GRACE: How do you know?

Grace unwraps the gun.

SUGAR: Please Grace. It's our birthday.

GRACE: Gun's cocked Trout an' finger's froggin' twitchin'. Who are ya?

TROUT: Fuck –

GRACE: Frog.

TROUT: Frog. Fuck –

GRACE: Frog.

TROUT: Frog. Fuck. Frog.

GRACE: Who are ya?

TROUT: Trout Stanley.

She nudges him.

TROUT: My name is Trout Stanley.

She nudges him again.

TROUT: Okay. Fuck –

GRACE: Frog.

TROUT: Frog. Fuck –

GRACE: Frog.

TROUT: Okay. Frog. Fuck. Frog. My name is Trout Stanley. I was born in a trailer in the woods not far from here between Misery Junction and Grizzly Alley. Truth. I swear on my sword, truth.

GRACE: How's the sword Sugar?

SUGAR: Worth the truth.

Grace gives him the nod.

TROUT: I grew up in silence save for the sound of a fire poppin' on
the stove-top, my mother's electric razor in the bathroom an'
the television on full tilt. Sometimes I called the television
Mother. My father spray-painted my bedroom wall when I was
six with the words *You were a mistake.*

My parents were prospectors. Mostly for other people's
jewels. My mother worked motel rooms, my father the men's
room. They could slip the ring off your weddin' finger while
you're sayin' your vows without anyone bein' the wiser. They
were smoother 'n silk, faster 'n leopards. I had no brothers an'
sisters. Mother an' Father would come home with their spoils
an' melt the gold and silver into different shapes, charms, pluck
the diamonds from their cheap settings, stare at candle hold-
ers for days at a time. Silent. Always silent. Save for the television: Mother.

My father develops a skin condition. He has to stop
wearin' clothes on his top half. Walks aroun' with a note from
the doctor sayin' it's okay that he's part naked. Pretty much
takes the wind outta their stealin' sails. So, one day, fires out,
faces hairless, they look at me an' they say: Unwanted son, we're
goin' an' we don' know if we'll ever be back. They leave with two
small toilet kits. It's my twelfth birthday. I have so many words
in my head but can't let them out, don' know how. Soap opera
is on. Guy havin' a flash of his dead wife an' he says sweatin',
cryin', slow-like: 'Come back. Come back. Come back to me.
Next time, not as a ghost … '

This is what I say to my parents. These are my firs' words.
But, it is too late. They are gone.

I stay in the trailer for the rest o' the year, grow a foot an'
grow a beard. Have a vegetable garden out back. Bear meat.
Moose meat. Partridge meat.

Day o' my thirteenth birthday. Sound of a car in the drive-
way. I press my face to the window. Thinkin' maybe it's Mother,

maybe it's Father. It's not. It's a cruiser. Cherries spin. Sirens go for a second – shortes', saddest opera in the world. I see the officer with his head bent at a sombre angle. He's the baritone. He's composin' himself. I know it's gonna be tragedy.

I put the kettle on. Small fire erupts. I put it out. Look out the window. He's still standin' there. Poor fuckin', froggin' guy. He's shakin'. He's cryin'. Doesn' know how to give me the news. Looks up to the heavens before makin' his sorry way to the door an' I see: he's not cryin', he's laughin'. Laughin' like a wild dog.

I take that in.

He knocks on the door. I open it, beard nearly to the floor. He says, 'Trout.' An' then he starts laughin' so hard he has to go back to his cruiser.

I take that in.

Gets his red-faced Junior to come out. While I'm standin' there blowin' in the wind like knickers, Junior opens his mouth but instead o' words, he starts laughin' too.

I take that in.

(Trout does a tiny cop show soundtrack.) Through a series of skillful manoeuvres memorized over years of watchin' cop shows, I manage to get them in the trailer. I lock the doors. I retire their weapons, strip them, cuff them and impersonate them on their cruiser radio. The Baritone gives me a letter written by his superior.

Trout opens his toilet kit. He pulls out a well-weathered letter. He does not refer to it once. By rote, by rote.

Dear Mr. Trout Stanley,

We regret to inform you that your parents, Mr. Sylvester Stanley and Mrs. Mayfair Stanley drowned on the first of May, of this past prospectin' season. It would appear that your parents, livin' off the land and whatever supplies they carried in their two small toilet kits, were attemptin' to scout out metal from the lake known as Diamond Lake or Lady Diamond

Lake. Witnesses say they saw your parents, a faintly bearded woman and a half-naked man standin' upright in a green canoe. Before witnesses could cry out to tell them to stop, your parents had placed their metal detectors on the surface of the Lady. Well, Trout, what can we say. She took them down in one fell flash. Canoe, toilet kits, metal detectors and all.

Cause of death is listed as electrocution.

We write to you because the nature of your parents' death has caused quite an uproar here at the Local Justice. When we practiced telling you the news, none of us could keep a straight face. That is why it comes a bit late and in the hands of two grossly underqualified juniors, one of whom is not even an officer but owes me a favour after an incident with my daughter and a display window.

Trout, well Trout, we also send our condolences to you for your name. We do not know how you will survive out in the world with a fish name. It is an unforgiving place and fish are low on the chain, my friend. Sorry, I have to take a small break from writing – I am laughing too hard.

Back to Sylvester and Mayfair Stanley. Since the Stanley deaths, your parents have been accused and convicted posthumously of the following: theft on 100 counts over the years 1979 to present. Amount stolen is estimated to be in and around one quarter of one million dollars. In these parts, son, namely the stretch between Misery Junction and Grizzly Alley, it appears there are no real laws. So we have pencilled some in and it turns out that despite what some might consider to be your tender age, in legalese, you are an adult. Your parents' crimes are now your crimes. You have no inheritance and no real legacy aside from ... Sorry, gonna have to take another break.

Your trial begins in one week.

We at the Local Justice send our sincerest condolences, and, as they say, we'll see you in court.

Sincerely,

Sherman and the Juniors.

I take that in.

The Juniors are now purple-faced wild dogs *(barkbarkbark)*, part laughin', part cryin', *(bark)* covered in goose pimples, penises whimperin' an' sucked into their doughy bodies. *(growls)* They disgust me.

My mother's electric razor is still in the bathroom. I take off my floor-length beard, leavin' a handsome moustache, an' cut my hair cop style. I put on the Baritone's sharp uniform an' silver sunglasses. I am what you might call cut out. More laughter. This time the choke-y type. I take their wallets, their weddin' rings, even their gold teeth. There are some tears at the teeth pullin'. Put the kettle on to comfort them but it starts a small fire. Melt the gold into different shapes, charms, pack my toilet kit, head for the door. But first I look into their wet eyes an' I laugh an' I laugh an' I laugh an' I laugh an' I laugh, choke-y type, cry-y type. Jus' as the trailer's about to go, flames hoppin' like hyperactive youngsters, I take a lingerin' look at the television an' say, 'Goodbye Mother.' Leave the Juniors chokin' chokin' cryin' cryin', get in the cruiser an' head as far away as I can from that place, God it feels good to talk.

... East. I decide to go east to train myself to be a visionary. On the way, I birth calves and see the earth from above. I discover the female persuasion an' I persuade. I star in an Egyptian soap opera until my character, a doctor, dies while trying to save the sick from a plague that has ravaged his city. I turn my eye to entrepreneurship. I mate snakes with cats an' call them cakes. Doesn' work, so I go into the boot business; your classic-cut rodeo styles probably came off my line. I make a fortune an' lose it all at the slots, high rollin', roulettin', pokerin' like a fool.

It is now the late eighties. There are ten thousand languages on this earth. I decide to take a vow o' silence. I only break it today, ten years later, when I firs' lay eyes on Sugar Ducharme. I also take a vow o' poverty. Beard's down to the ground. Wearin' the Baritone's uniform. Silver sunglasses too. I'm playin' my cello in a town square that sits perfect on the Tropic o' Capricorn. In the desert, if you stay in one place long enough, the sand'll bury ya whether ya like it or not. The one cake that survived the litter is dancin' below me. We're hungry an' thirsty an' tryin' to scare up some coin for a bed for the night. Been playin' for days. Sun's cookin' us. Fingers are near bleedin'. The cake is cryin'. Sand is up to our knees. Man walks by. Tosses a penny. Misses the toilet kit. I reach down to pick it up an' feel this lump right here *(touches his heart)* —

SUGAR: Your heart was broken.

TROUT: Went to the doctor fearin' the worst —

GRACE: Cancer.

SUGAR: Cancer o' the broken heart.

TROUT: The lump was my twin.

Grace and Sugar gasp.

TROUT: My unformed twin —

Grace and Sugar gasp.

TROUT: — that had somehow gotten mixed up in my flesh, in my blood, an' never grown. My whole life I knew: somethin's missin' —

SUGAR: Somethin's missin' —

TROUT: Somethin's not right —

SUGAR: Somethin's not right —

TROUT: No matter how far east I got —

SUGAR: *(whispers)* No matter how far east —

TROUT: It was him. It was my twin that was missin'. My unformed twin.

SUGAR: I'll make a figurine of him.

GRACE: How d'you know it was a him?

TROUT: Instinct.

GRACE/SUGAR: We got that.

SUGAR: Some places way far north where it's only daylight, the people are full o' souls. At least six or seven of 'em an' they come in the shape o' tiny humans an' they can live anywhere in your body. Roof o' your mouth, in your eye, big toe, under your heart.

GRACE: This was a lump, not a soul.

SUGAR/TROUT: It was a soul.

GRACE: Still doesn' explain what you want with us —

SUGAR: With me —

GRACE: Froggin' twitchin' trigger finger Trout.

TROUT: When I stumbled onto your place, peered into the window an' saw sweet Sugar Cereal standin' in sorrow in the mornin' sun, there was liftoff.

SUGAR: Liftoff.

TROUT: Liftoff. I love your sister an' I will not go back to what life was without her. I will never come down Grace Ducharme ... When she told me you were twins, I knew this love was some kind o' divine workin'. Don't you see, I, we were meant to find you ... May we please stay for your birthday party?

Long pause. Sugar looks to Grace. Grace looks to Sugar. They stare at Trout. Pause. Grace and Sugar confer.

SUGAR: He's rubbing his unformed twin.

Trout is rubbing his unformed twin.

SUGAR: Please, for me.

Grace places her hand above Trout's heart. She feels. Lingers. Withdraws.

SUGAR: Grace. It's exactly our birthday. This very second. Happy birthday Grace.

GRACE: Happy birthday Sugar.

SUGAR/GRACE: Happy birthday Duckling.

TROUT: Happy birthday.

Grace puts down the gun.

GRACE: You can stay.

Blackout.

everything looks

good from

here

Act Two

Scene Seven

Birthday party. Heart is playing at full volume. Trout and Sugar — her party hat crooked, a streamer tied around her neck — dance beside the record player. A bottle of booze slightly emptied, remains of a roast, some soda cans. Grace is dead sober. She addresses Trout while Sugar continues to dance — drunkenly, a comet in her own universe.

GRACE: She's been listenin' to that same record since high school. Ya'd think it would've driven me crazy by now, but it hasn't. Ya'd think the record'd be all scratched up. But it isn't. Sometimes I think Sugar's protected. Sugar's protected by the gods, ya know … The Holies, how they loved her. Like she was the Third Comin'. The Be All. The End All. Sugar Cereal. Sometimes, they'd jus' look at her, waitin' to see what she might do next. An' there she'd be. Doin' nothin' at all. But it fascinated them. Still a newborn in their eyes … Everything gets ranked Trout. Everywhere. It's inevitable.

TROUT: It's the animal kingdom.

GRACE: It's life. It's love. Winners on top. Losers on the bottom. *(Grace cracks open a soda.)* Are you a good man Trout — ?

Sugar approaches — interrupting.

SUGAR: *(raising her glass throughout, Grace occasionally filling it)* This is the best party I've ever been to. This is the only party I've ever been to. 'Side from the prom, but that doesn't count 'cause that was a joke on me by Tommy 'the Joystick' Larue an' his mean inbred rotting spirit, but doesn' matter now, he's dead to me — rigor mortis, eyes open.

I thought surprise was extinct in these parts. Who would know that on a day when I should've been bludgeoned, when I should've joined our dearly departed in their restless state, I would instead find love. I would find love in the form of a man with a soul that is the most beautiful colour red, a man with a soul that tastes like the purest o' water, a man with a soul that smells of everything that's awake an' alive: dirt, crustaceans, the milky way — a man with a soul that has orgasms.

I've been off the map too long, dear ones; I've been a tumbleweed rollin' across my own untravelled highway — secretly wishin' for a head-on.

Grace, you've been my constant companion since we were conceived in the Holy Mother's womb — except from nine to five weekdays. I offer you this birthday present.

Sugar retrieves a perfectly wrapped box, hands it to Grace; Grace starts to open it.

We all know that you are duly represented in many public forums, but sometimes it is good to see how we might appear to the ones who love us most. You are mighty an' you have taught me *(looks at Trout)* ... almost everything.

Grace pulls out a figurine of herself, handles it, quizzical.

TROUT: Wow.

SUGAR: I hope you wish us well, Trout and I — on our unplanned an' ill-defined trip that could lead to nowhere. Nowhere or bust, I've finally found my purpose Grace: to join Trout in headin' north, to join him in findin' his parents' death place. That's what I'm good at. Remember? I've finally caught up with my life an' what it's supposed to be.

Sugar kisses Trout on the lips.

SUGAR: I love you an' I love your unformed twin.

Sugar passes out. Trout doesn't catch her.

½ GHOST , ½ DUCKLING,

PRONE TO HAUNTING

Scene Eight

Sugar is passed out on the couch. Trout circles her like a furrow-browed, gentle-hearted hawk.

TROUT: Shouldn' we put her in the shower?

GRACE: She hates showers.

TROUT: A splash o' cold water.

GRACE: She hates to wash. She hates all forms o' washin'. She's been wearin' that track suit for ten years. It's our dead mother's.

TROUT: She told me.

Trout shakes her a little. Nothing. Grace shakes her — with vigour. Nothing.

GRACE: She'll be fine. It's happened before. Should've seen her at the double wake. She wet her pants. Should've seen her at the prom — she bled all over the back of her dress. Her days. She started on her days. That night. Passed out on the rec room sofa at Tommy 'the Joystick' Larue's, poor thing. So.

TROUT: So. Coffee, sometimes coffee —

GRACE: She hates coffee.

TROUT: Jus' the smell.

GRACE: She hates the smell. She hates all hot liquid.

TROUT: Guess we'll let 'er sleep it off.

GRACE: Prob'ly best.

Trout strokes Sugar's hair, her face.

GRACE: Shouldn' stroke her when she sleeps. Might disturb her.

TROUT: Oh.

He stops.

TROUT: *(lifting a bottle of liquor)* Mind if I – ?

GRACE: Go right ahead.

He drains the bottle.

TROUT: Takes the edge off.

GRACE: The edge.

TROUT: The edge o' life, generally, I find it sharp.

GRACE: Me too.

TROUT: D'ya have any hobbies?

GRACE: Not really.

TROUT: Nothin' at all. Crochet, stargazin' –

GRACE: Nope.

TROUT: The tuba –

GRACE: Nope. Nothin'.

TROUT: Do ya like martial arts – ?

GRACE: No.

TROUT: Me neither. I find them sudden. Do ya like horses?

GRACE: Not really.

TROUT: Do ya read?

GRACE: Sugar does.

TROUT: You don'.

GRACE: No. Don't see the point. I've looked death in the face. I've
looked loss in the face. I've looked God in the face. Why pick
up a book?

TROUT: … We should tidy.

GRACE: We should.

They tidy a bit. Grace stops. Trout doesn't.

GRACE: Dynamite, eh.

TROUT: What?

GRACE: My zip-up. Lates' summer trend. A T-shirt an' shorts in
one quick zip-up.

TROUT: Zip up.

GRACE: Zip down.

TROUT: Zip up.

GRACE: Zip down … Sugar tell ya I'm the billboard girl at the Four Corners?

TROUT: Ah –

GRACE: Gets her down. But I say we get the face we deserve in this life and surely she got hers for a reason.

TROUT: Maybe she did mention it.

GRACE: Sit down.

TROUT: I'm –

GRACE: Here. Make yourself at home.

TROUT: Thanks.

He sits.

GRACE: So. You haven't seen the billboard.

TROUT: What billboard?

GRACE: The one at the Four Corners.

TROUT: No. I haven't seen the billboard.

GRACE: Went up this mornin'. Minutes later there was a crush o' people at Stan's Western Gear an' Shootin' Range.

TROUT: At Stan's –

GRACE: He called me. At the Dump. He was ecstatic, beside himself. Bigger 'n Boxin' Day, he said, bigger 'n Boxin' Day.

TROUT: Is 'at so?

GRACE: So as so can be. Stan gave me the zip-up an' the boots as a token o' his respect.

TROUT: Nice boots.

TROUT/GRACE: Classic cut.

They laugh.

TROUT/GRACE: Rodeo style.

They laugh.

GRACE: Now I want ya to imagine a camo backdrop, so I fade into it, fade into the scenery, like a huntress. 'Cept this. *(points at her eyes)* I got this look in my eye. Somethin' between red-hot sexy an' I'm-gonna-squeeze-your-balls-blue dangerous –

TROUT: Sugar –

GRACE: She's out … 'Look out Deer, look out Moose. We got rifles an' we're lookin' for youse.' That's the slogan.

TROUT: Wow.

GRACE: Who could forget it?

TROUT: No one.

GRACE: Between you an' me, before I agreed to do it, before I agreed to be the Four Corners Billboard Girl, I asked Stan if Sugar could be in it with me. You know: the Ducharme sisters. Twins. But he said no. He said she jus' didn't have the good fortune I had, if ya know what I mean. An' he didn't say it quite as delicate as that. Breaks my heart Trout. Even more than it breaks hers.

Grace is suddenly very still. She scans the horizon; her eyes rest on Trout. She stares. Trout begins to squirm. Finally.

TROUT: What're you doin'? Grace.

GRACE: A re-enactment. O' the billboard. Since ya missed it. Whaddaya think?

TROUT: It's, ah, ironic.

GRACE: Exactly. You're smart Trout. Let's have a little fun –

TROUT: Ah –

Grace rummages through a drawer in the kitchen.

GRACE: You haven' heard about us.

TROUT: No.

GRACE: We're savages, freaks o' the underbrush.

TROUT: Lucky me.

GRACE: Lucky you.

They laugh. Grace pulls a rope from the drawer, lassoes Trout. He struggles. She starts tying him up.

GRACE: What're ya made of Trout Stanley – ?

TROUT: Blood and bone, baby, blood and bone. Wait –

GRACE: Trust me.

TROUT: Why should I?

GRACE: I'm almos' your sister.

TROUT: Don't see the point o' the rope.

GRACE: You will.

TROUT: Some kind o' birthday party game.

GRACE: Yeah. You like games?

TROUT: Depends on the game. You're strong.

GRACE: Someone's gotta be –

TROUT: Ow –

GRACE: Run the Dump all by my lonesome –

TROUT: Ow –

GRACE: There's bears out there. Sometimes we come to blows –

TROUT: Ow –

GRACE: An' the ravens –

TROUT: F– Ow –

GRACE: They're fatter 'n churches –

TROUT: Ow.

GRACE: Oops. But they know their queen. Done.

She finishes tying him up. Sips her soda.

TROUT: Can ya untie me now?

GRACE: No. I had a killer day today.

TROUT: I'm sorry to hear that.

GRACE: I've done some shameful things in my life.

TROUT: We all have. D'ya think ya could at least loosen these?

Grace roars.

TROUT: No.

GRACE: They call me the Lion Queen.

TROUT: Is 'at so?

She roars again.

GRACE: Lions like fish.

TROUT: I can see that.

She roars.

TROUT: Big cat.

She roars again.

TROUT: Little fish.

She roars. He roars. Grace kisses him.

TROUT: Ah —

She kisses him again.

TROUT: Lub a dub —

Kissing.

TROUT: Ah, a few years ago, I would've been really into this —

Kissing.

TROUT: Ya know, ropes, twins, a birthday party —

Kissing.

TROUT: But I'm past all that.

She kisses him again.

TROUT: I love your sister, I love your sister. *(looking at Sugar)* Sugar —

GRACE: She's out.

TROUT: Can't we do somethin' — ?

GRACE: We can do anythin' —

Grace kisses him again.

TROUT: Really, a few years ago –

Kisses him.

TROUT: Oh God –

Kisses him.

TROUT: A few years ago –

Kisses him.

TROUT: Oh. Sugar.

Kisses him.

TROUT: Mus' be tough.

GRACE: What Trout Stanley? What's tough?

TROUT: Bein' lef' behin'. Here. To run the Dump. Is it really a place fit for a queen?

GRACE: Garbage is tea leaves, is tarot cards, is crystal balls. That's what the Holy Father said. An' he was right. I know everything that happens in this town Trout Stanley. Garbage tells me everything. Garbage is the mos' truthful story I ever heard.

TROUT: What about the stink, doesn' it get to ya? Get in your clothes, in your skin, your eyes?

GRACE: The stink. It's humanity. An' people who're scared o' the stink are scared o' humanity. I for one am not. Sugar thinks I'm vain. That all I care about is this. My mane, my dynamite outfits, my classic-cut rodeo-style cowboy boots. Bullroar.

90

Sure, sometimes bein' in the Boutique Christmas catalogues goes to my head. Boutique head, you know. Billboard head. Floatin' a little through town. 'Specially when I catch a glimpse o' myself in the backroom at the SuperSavers or pinned up in the fire station, guys crowded around my calendar. I like it. I like the attention. I like bein' liked. I like bein' looked at. But I don' need it. I got other things. Other dreams. Other secrets. I got a million, Trout. Sugar an' her tragedies. She thinks I don' know the grisly side o' life. Well I do. Whatever's happened to her has happened to me too.

TROUT: Till now.

GRACE: I love one thing. An' it's Sugar. Sugar's my life … Ten years ago, the Holy Mother was struck by a fever. She had a temperature of 106 degrees. That's hotter'n India Trout, hotter'n Greece, *(toys with him)* hotter'n the fire in your pants –

TROUT: Sugar –

GRACE: She's out. The Holy Mother lay in her bed. Burnin' like a coil. Holy Father wouldn' let the doctors in. Sayin' they're all quacks. So we watched her day an' night. On rotation. Gave her ice baths, ice water, love. She jus' thrashed in her sheets sayin' weird, sometimes terrible, sometimes beautiful things, feverish things. She even spoke to our dear dead Ducklin' – though she didn' call her that. She called her Angel. *Angel.* Sugar never heard it; neither did the Holy Father. Jus' me. Angel.
  Durin' the day, the Holy Father an' I would go to the Dump. Try to keep livin'. Normal life. Well I hate Normal an' I'm pretty sure Normal hates me. We come home the afternoon of our twentieth birthday an' there's Sugar sittin' on the Holy Mother's bed, glowin' like a jack-o'-lantern.

TROUT: Jesus –

GRACE: The Holy Mother had died jus' moments before. Sugar's the las' to touch her; the heat spreads through her like the Tropics an' it fills her with a low-burnin' orange. She looks like a leaf held upside the sun. Can see all her veins. Her eyes are fireballs.

The Holy Father is come over with a terrible grief. He starts to yowl an' shake. Suddenly he takes off into the Pines. Are we gonna lose him too? Whole town forms a search party, out in their bug suits, flashlights sweepin' like meteor showers, cops twistin' their moustaches into pipe cleaners, whole teams o' dogs, whole teams o' everyone, shoutin', sniffin', scourin', eyes fixed to the groun' ... an' then Sugar comes between us with a superior quiet — partin' the Red Sea an' leadin' us, our Laura Secord, leadin' us to him, to the Holy Father. An' there he was, split by lightnin'. Like an axe to wood. Split perfect in two. Standin' under the tallest tree. Tree an echo o' what he is. Split. Perfect. Funny thing is, it was the cleares' night o' the year. Not a cloud in the sky ... An' there we were, made orphans in a night.

This is why we make promises Trout. 'Cause promises give us somethin' to believe in, somethin' to hold onto. Somethin' sure. Otherwise we're all jus' circlin' the earth wonderin' where it's safe to land ...

Night before the Holy Mother dies she makes me swear on everything that I will protect Sugar with my life. 'Promise that you will take care of your sister Grace, for she is prized. Between you, me, an' the above an' beyond, if we had to pin a ribbon on one o' ya, it'd be Sugar. Sugar has a future.' An' what do I have, I asked the Holy Mother, her eyes flutterin' like tired butterflies. 'You have Sugar,' she said, 'you have Sugar.' That's the last conversation we had. Some might say my mother was cruel. I say she was jus' sayin' it like it is.

An' that's what I'm doin' Trout Stanley: I'm protectin' Sugar, I'm protectin' Sugar with my life. She's an easy target. She's the perfect prey. An' people who take advantage, they're stacked in the woods.

TROUT: Are they?

GRACE: I know your kind: Mr. Mud Hut. Driftin' through town. No fixed address. Traveller o' many faces. I've dreamt o' that. Bein' nothin' but a room number. Belongin' to nowhere an' then checkin' out. You have no idea what it's like to be deathbed responsible for every wakin' moment of another person's life. Now ... tell me you love me.

TROUT: What?

GRACE: Tell me you love me.

TROUT: But I don't.

GRACE: Tell me you love me.

TROUT: I, I don't.

GRACE: Yes you do.

TROUT: No. I don't.

GRACE: You love me.

TROUT: I don't.

GRACE: You love me.

TROUT: No. I don't.

GRACE: Tell me.

TROUT: No.

GRACE: Tell me.

TROUT: No.

GRACE: Tell me.

TROUT: I don't –

GRACE: You love me.

TROUT: I don't.

GRACE: Like lightnin'.

TROUT: No.

GRACE: *(hits her heart)* Right here.

TROUT: No.

GRACE: Firs' sight.

TROUT: I can't lie. I never do.

GRACE: Everybody does.

TROUT: I just, I can't, I don't, I never lie.

GRACE: You should learn how.

TROUT: This is exactly why I took a vow o' silence.

Grace gets the shotgun.

TROUT: I'm startin' to feel unsafe Grace. Sugar –

GRACE: She's out.

TROUT: You've already got me tied up; I don't see why you need the gun.

GRACE: Extra security.

TROUT: Seems a bit over the top.

GRACE: That's me, that's my style – Grace Ducharme, a bit over the top, pow pow.

TROUT: How-how. I'm a white flag Grace.

GRACE: Are ya?

TROUT: I'd wave if I could but I can't. Please.

GRACE: Pow.

TROUT: Please.

GRACE: I'm a perfect shot.

TROUT: I'm a perfect target. Please.

GRACE: Don't beg.

TROUT: This was supposed to be a birthday party.

She points the gun at him. Trout shushes his twin.

TROUT: Sh, sh, it's okay, it's okay –

GRACE: One last thing –

The phone rings. Shrill as a siren. They scream.

TROUT: Sugar —

GRACE: She's out. *(She walks over to him.)* Wha' do you know about the Scrabble Champ Stripper?

TROUT: Nothin'.

GRACE: What do you know about the Scrabble Champ Stripper?

TROUT: Nothin', I know nothin' —

GRACE: Nothin' —

TROUT: Nothin', swear on my sword, nothin'.

GRACE: Nothin' —

TROUT: Nothin'. Truth. I never lie.

GRACE: No one never lies.

TROUT: Except me. I never lie. I never lie. If I could lie, don't you think I'd be lyin' right now?

GRACE: There's a killer on the loose.

TROUT: She's missin', she's not dead —

GRACE: How do you know — ?

TROUT: I don't know. This is my point: I don't know anything. Let me tell ya how this looks from my end, Lion Queen. We have been walkin' for years. Penniless mutes, failed visionaries.

Tryin' to get home. We have met every kind o' human face. Almos' there, we're tired. We're thirsty. We need to catch our breath. We stumble onto this place; it's the only one aroun'. We peer in the window thinkin' maybe the folk who live here'll put us up, feed us sausages and lend us their bathwater. Maybe we'll feel comfort. Sometimes, all a man wants is comfort.

But no. I'm in eternal love. I'm at a birthday party. I'm bein' tied up. I'm bein' kissed. I'm bein' held hostage, at gunpoint, by my Sugar's twin – who, by the way, looks nothin' froggin' like her. All fair game. It's an unpredictable universe, I know that. But then I'm bein' accused o' murder. Now this is uncalled for. I would never harm a woman so long as my blood signature is Trout Stanley.

But I don't think that's your concern Grace Ducharme. That's just a decoy, the huntress's ceramic birdie, the Lion Queen's trick call. Pow pow. You're shootin' the sky. Well, here's what's fallin' from it: love. Love. Love makes us, period.

This lowest on the chain o' life, this bottom-feedin' fish, this mistake has one miracle, an' that one miracle is my love for Sugar Ducharme. Bull's eye. Shoot me dead an' even then we'll be together. That is why, Grace Ducharme, that is why I cannot lie, that is why I cannot tell you that (*Sugar wakes up*) I love you.

Grace kisses Trout furiously.

GRACE: You love me.

SUGAR: No Grace. Trout.

TROUT: Sugar.

SUGAR: Grace.

GRACE: Sugar, wait –

SUGAR: *(to Grace)* ... You steal everything.

GRACE: It's not what ya think –

SUGAR: It's what I saw. Please God, scoop out my mouldy eyes –

Sugar tries to leave. Grace stops her. Holds her still.

GRACE: Stop –

SUGAR: Every promise, every dotted line, every moment we've shared, includin' our nine months together on an indescribable planet with our dear dead Ducklin', is a lie. You, my sister, are a lie.

GRACE: Stop it.

SUGAR: I had so much love in me it was a bomb waitin' to go off.

Turns to leave.

GRACE: You are not leavin' this house.

SUGAR: Oh yes, I am. I'm joinin' Ducklin'. As she punished us for bein' greedy in love, I'll join her, makin' the punishment double what it was.

Sugar frees herself.

SUGAR: *(exiting)* What's your purpose Grace? What's yours?

Sugar locks eyes with Trout.

TROUT: Truth –

SUGAR: No.

She leaves by the front door.

TROUT: Sugar. Sugar. Sugar —

GRACE: Oh my God —

TROUT: Stop her Grace. Sugar —

GRACE: She hasn't left the house in ten years, oh my God, Sugar —

TROUT: Sugar —

GRACE: Sugar. Sugar Cereal —

TROUT: Sweet Sugar —

GRACE: Sugar Cereal, Sugar, come back —

TROUT: Get her, go —

GRACE: Sugar, please —

Grace chases her out. Trout is alone. We see his hands working feverishly to free himself from the ropes. Blackout.

Scene Nine

Midnight. Trout is clawingly desperate, exhausted. Grace returns. Breathless.

GRACE: She's gone.

TROUT: I know.

GRACE: Not jus' Sugar.

TROUT: Whaddaya mean?

GRACE: Sometimes work jus' takes over, takes a hold o' ya like a boa constrictor.

TROUT: I don't understand.

Grace turns on the television. She flips through the channels.

NEWS: ... No suspects and no new leads in the mysterious disappearance of a local Chetwynd woman *(flip)* ... Authorities are losing hope ... *(flip)* Went missing three nights ago after her shift at Rodeo ... *(flip)* Today was her thirtieth birthday... *(flip)* As we are nearing midnight ... *(flip)* Every home in the area has a candle burning ... *(flip)* Everyone waiting, hoping and praying ... *(flip)* Angel, Angel *(flip)* Come back. Come back. Next time, not as a ghost.

Grace turns off the television. She paces.

TROUT: When I came here this mornin' –

GRACE: Shush it, I'm thinkin'–

TROUT: When I came here this mornin', Sugar was set to hang herself.

GRACE: What?

TROUT: Sugar was standin' on this very chair, this very rope hung 'round her neck ... Grace?

GRACE: What?

TROUT: Why did Sugar wanna die?

GRACE: I don't know, I don't know ...

At the window, spectral light.

It's twilight Trout Stanley, twilight. The end o' light. Can't tell shadow from substance. Earth from air. God from demon. It's a trick light. Everything comes outta hiding. The elk, the wolves, the bats, the grizzlies, the ghosts. The ditch dwellers. The world is jus' pairs o' eyes, followin' ya, yellow, unflinchin', darin' ya with a stare. There's peril every mile, Trout Stanley, peril every mile. Then the sun, what's left of it, sinks so fast an' we see: there's only seconds between heaven an' hell. There's only seconds till the world bares its teeth an' shows ya what it really is: hungry an' unforgivin'. We both know, if given the chance, the world'll lick ya clean to the bone.

We both know, soon it'll be dark, an' —

TROUT/GRACE: — the dark plays for keeps.

GRACE: I gotta find her. *(flashlight, shotgun, heads for the front door)* I gotta find her, I gotta —

TROUT: Let me go with you.

GRACE: No.

TROUT: We'll go together.

GRACE: We won't.

TROUT: Why?

GRACE: I'm gonna save her. Alone.

Grace stops at the mirror, adjusts her hair, her makeup, her zip-up.

GRACE: Me. Grace Ducharme. Lion Queen.

Grace at the front door.

TROUT: I can see it from a mile away.

GRACE: What? See what?

TROUT: You're a woman who's never been touched.

GRACE: That's a lie.

TROUT: Is it?

Grace circles him, presses her face to his.

TROUT: Peace peace.

Grace steps back, heads for the door.

TROUT: You should fix your —

GRACE: What — ?

TROUT: Hair. Could be a headliner.

Grace considers this. She spins around. Trout trips her. Over the course of the night, he has freed himself from the ropes that bound him to the chair. They struggle.

GRACE: What the – ?

TROUT: Frog.

Struggle.

GRACE: How did you – ?

TROUT: Cop shows.

Trout does a tiny cop-show soundtrack.

GRACE: Get off me Trout Stanley –

TROUT: No.

GRACE: Ow.

TROUT: Oops.

He manages to get the shotgun.

GRACE: I don't see what you possibly hope to accomplish –

TROUT: Sit down. Here.

She does. He puts the gun aside, starts to tie her up.

GRACE: I tied you up 'cause I thought you were the Scrabble Champ Stripper killer. Same certainly can't be said o' me.

TROUT: I disagree.

He tightens the ropes.

GRACE: Let me go.

TROUT: No.

GRACE: Every second you waste on me you lose on your precious
Sugar.

TROUT: I'll find her.

GRACE: Will ya?

TROUT: Yes.

GRACE: We all have our day o' reckonin' Trout Stanley.

TROUT: We sure do. There.

He finishes tying her up. Trout heads for the door.

GRACE: You'll need the flashlight.

TROUT: No I won't.

Trout retrieves the shotgun.

TROUT: Does this thing even work?

GRACE: I didn' test it.

TROUT: Where'd you get it?

GRACE: Tommy 'the Joystick' Larue. Shoot the roof.

TROUT: No.

GRACE: It's my house.

TROUT: So?

GRACE: Thought you wanted to see if it works.

TROUT: Changed my mind. I hate guns.

He drops the gun. The gun goes off. The roast explodes.

TROUT: I shot the roast I shot the roast I shot the roast –

Trout is stunned, distracted, by his butchery. Grace frantically unties the ropes.

TROUT: I shot the roast. I shot the roast. Sorry. Sorry. I'm so sorry. I shot the roast Grace. I shot the roast.

GRACE: It works.

TROUT: It works.

They laugh.

GRACE: Oh my God.

TROUT: What.

GRACE: Your foot is bleeding.

TROUT: Oh my God.

He looks down. It's not. Grace leaps for Trout — her hands are unbound.

TROUT: Fuck —

GRACE: Frog.

TROUT: You're good —

GRACE: I love to win —

TROUT: Me too —

Trout gets on top of Grace.

GRACE: I'll take you to her.

TROUT: How?

GRACE: Before, I was blind, I was blind with worry. But the huntress is back. You need me Trout.

TROUT: I found her once. I'll find her again.

GRACE: You can't leave me here alone, tied up.

TROUT: You're scared.

GRACE: There is somethin' else at work.

TROUT: Wha' do you mean?

GRACE: Take me.

TROUT: Tell me.

GRACE: When I pulled in an' went aroun' the back o' the truck to get my lunch pail, there she was. There she was in all o' her sparkly regalia.

TROUT: Who?

GRACE: The Scrabble Champ Stripper.

TROUT: No.

GRACE: The Scrabble Champ Stripper. Musta brought the corpse home. But when I went out just now, to look for Sugar, she was gone. Vanished.

Sudden sunrise. Blinds Trout. The front door flies open. Sugar enters wearing the Scrabble Champ Stripper's rodeo outfit. She is glowing like a jack-o'-lantern.

I NEED A DUMPTRUCK TO UNLOAD MY HEAD

Scene Ten

Trout and Grace stare at Sugar. The glow dying down.

SUGAR: Trout.

TROUT: Sugar.

SUGAR: Grace.

GRACE: Sugar.

SUGAR: Why does everything around us die?

GRACE: There's lots still standin'. A whole world out there.

SUGAR: Ever since I was young, I've been so full o' love. I'd go to the store to get a popsicle or gum or a comic book an' Stella behin' the counter would say, 'Bye Sugar. Have a good day.' An' I'd say, 'You too Stella. *(whispers)* I love you.' I'd walk to school, books in hand, an' the guys at the gas station they'd yell out, 'Hey Sugar, don' study too hard.' An' I'd shout back, 'I won't guys. Promise. *(whispers)* I love you.' I'd be buyin' our groceries, gettin' my change, an' Randolph would say, 'Goodbye Sugar, have a killer night.' An' I'd say, 'You too Randolph. Killer. *(whispers)* I love you.'

Always under my breath. No one could hear it. It was a secret. It was a million secrets.

Then it spread from people to animals. Fish, birds, ants, blackflies, squirrels. When the squirrel shootin' started, you can imagine how tragic it was given that I was so full of *I love yous*. My heart broke. Holies died the next year. My heart broke again. Didn' know my heart could break a third time.

Grace, did you tell Tommy 'the Joystick' Larue to invite me to the prom as a joke?

GRACE: That was a long time ago Sugar.

SUGAR: Grace, do you know that people call here all day jus' to listen to me say hello an' then they hang up 'cause they find it so funny. I can hear them laughin' on the other end o' the line … I made ya a figurine o' yourself Grace, 'cause I figured that yourself's all you'd wanna look at anyway.

GRACE: That's not true. I like lookin' at lots o' things.

SUGAR: Like what?

GRACE: Like … I dunno.

Grace is still for a moment, directionless. Sugar picks up the gun.

GRACE: Sugar. Careful now Sugar Cereal.

TROUT: It works.

GRACE: Shush it.

TROUT: I shot the roast.

GRACE: Shush it.

TROUT: I'm jus' sayin' –

GRACE: Shush it –

TROUT: It works; I can't lie –

GRACE: Shush it –

TROUT: It's a problem sometimes –

GRACE: Shush it.

Sugar throws the gun out the front door.

SUGAR: When I lef' here, I found the Scrabble Champ Stripper, lyin' face up in the back o' your truck lef' there like a piece o' lumber, like a spare tire, like a bag o' salt.

TROUT: Jesus —

SUGAR: I dragged her through the Pines, fought off the bears an' the ravens till I reached the Holies' burial place an' I dug an' I dug an' I thought: this is the bes' birthday present I can give you Grace. Maybe with this, we'll break the death spell.

TROUT: The death spell.

SUGAR: We were supposed to be holy, we were supposed to be three, but, instead my sister, it's just you and me. Ever since the Holies died, every year, every birthday, someone dies who's exactly our age. An' every year, every birthday, Grace finds her body.

TROUT: You find her body. Every year, every birthday.

SUGAR: It's a spell an' it's a spell we had to break.

TROUT: That's what you were tryin' to do this mornin'.

SUGAR: Little did I know, I didn' have to.
       When I was done with my gruesome mortal work, I stood there for a long time. Catchin' my breath. Reflectin' on our life.
       I buried the Holy Mother's track suit Grace. Her slippers too. Just as you wanted. Stood there, naked as the dawn, an' then decided on this. *(runs hands along rodeo outfit)* She will not be forgotten, whoever she was …

I thought I knew my own home as well as I know my own face, as well as I know yours *(looks at Grace)*. I didn't. I don't. I only needed to travel one mile to see it for what it really is.

You would think that bein' in the presence o' the Scrabble Champ Stripper would jus' prove the death spell true. But no, I have learned twice too often, firs' with the Holy Mother, melted into a fever before my eyes, an' then with the Holy Father, cleaved by grief — a corpse tells a different story. Doesn't it Grace?

GRACE: Yes Sugar.

SUGAR: When you're that close to death, a line is drawn. You cannot go back. Jus' like in love, the world as you knew it before is —

SUGAR/TROUT: — irretrievable.

SUGAR: Exactly.
Death. This is something that you know as well as I do Grace.

GRACE: Yes Sugar.

SUGAR: This is something that you were only reminded of today, for the firs' time in ten years.
Grace. Have you been lyin' about findin' dead bodies every year since the Holies died? Have you been lyin' about the death spell to keep me here, to keep me scared?

TROUT: Tell the truth now Grace. Truth.

GRACE: Truth. Perfect mornin', perfect lunch, a perfect day Sugar. Our birthday. There is nothin' I am more proud of than bein' your twin. I decide to take a walk around the Dump. I remember the Holy Father sayin', 'There's nothin' quite like seein' things from the ground level Grace. That's when you know the truth. By bein' in it. Got to be in the garbage sometimes Grace. Got to be in the garbage to know the garbage.'

I leave the 'dozer at the office. Pictures o' the Holies smilin' straight on the wall. Everything neat. Everything jus' so. Blue sky, brown earth, garbage. Tuck my coveralls into my boots an' walk. Fresh furniture piled high since the mine closed. Fridges, their doors pulled off, lined up like beauty contestants. An' the most perfect section of all, my pride an' joy, the residential, black bag upon black bag winkin' at me in the afternoon sun. I stand back an' look at it: a perfect pyramid. An' I'm its builder.

I decide to climb it – for a birthday treat. I'll have a view o' the whole town. I'll see all of it for both of us. I'll have so much to tell ya when I get home. I'll see the end o' time. I climb – never done this before – an' with every step, I think about kings, kings buried with everything that was theirs in life. Their queens, their cats, their children, their horses, their soldiers, their golden possessions – all crossin' over, joinin' 'em in death. What a greedy lot, the kings, I think, like a drownin' man pullin' his saviour down to join 'im in the deep. It is then that I swear, it is then that I promise, today, this day, I will end the death spell. I will never lie to you again Sugar. I will not pull you down into the deep. The death spell is done, dotted, done. Lucky thirty. Fresh decade. In the clear. We will be free. You, you will be free.

That's when I stumble on somethin' Sugar, an' I fall flat, landin' face to face with somethin', landin' face to face with a woman. Right there like a mirror, top o' my perfect pyramid, highes' point in all o' Tumbler Ridge. She's grey as a mouse coat; can barely tell she has eyes, she's so swollen – like one o' your tragedies. Glitter makeup on her cheeks, mouth open, as though she's about to ask for the time. I pick myself up real fast an' hear this thuddin'. Footsteps. It's the footsteps o' God an' they're comin' to get me. I'm gonna lose consciousness; I'm gonna get pulled down into the deep an' never be found. I'm gonna vanish too. Jus' then a raven swoops by, screeches me awake.

I run back to the office, the Holies now crooked, now frownin' on the wall, piles o' garbage everywhere, pyramid wrecked, our perfect day gone. I get in the truck to come home to ya, hit the gas pedal. I can barely see the road. I can barely see the road 'cause I can't get the snapshot of her out o' my head. She keeps lookin' more an' more like you Sugar. More an' more every second, as the snapshot develops – perfect in my brain. It won't go away . . . I see before me, stark an' plain, a world without you in it. An' I don' know if it's a world that I can live in.

Firs' thing I ever heard was my own heartbeat. I can't tell you the echo. Next thing I heard was yours.

I'm sorry.

SUGAR: What?

GRACE: I'm sorry. I lied Sugar, all those years, I lied.

SUGAR: I los' ten years in the outside world. I don' know what you lost.

GRACE: You. Have I lost you?

SUGAR: We had our share o' sufferin' an' now we're in the clear. I forgive you Grace. *(kisses Grace)* Curse closed.

GRACE: I spend my days orderin' the things lef' behin' – that can get your mind racin' . . . I know what my purpose is now. It's to be the las' one standin', the las' one standin' in a dyin' town. One day, even the sun'll burn out, but I'll still be here. I'm the one who knows the stories. I'm the one who knows what's happened. Better 'n anyone. It's in my clothes, my skin, my eyes.

Sugar turns to Trout. She takes his hand.

TROUT: Wait. There's somethin' I need to confess.

SUGAR: Oh no.

TROUT: Two nights ago –

SUGAR: No –

TROUT: Two nights ago –

SUGAR: Please –

TROUT: I broke in here an' ate your roast an' drank some booze an' sniffed your slippers.

SUGAR: That's okay.

TROUT: Come with me Sugar.

SUGAR: North.

TROUT: North. I love you.

GRACE: He does. Sugar.

SUGAR: Yeah.

GRACE: What's it like?

SUGAR: What?

GRACE: Love.

SUGAR: It's like two snails. Meetin' for the firs' time. On a beautiful day.

GRACE: … Garbage is callin'. I can't keep it waitin'. Better start gettin' freshened up.

TROUT: It's firs' light.

GRACE: Still, with that new billboard, could be a whole lot o' passers through. You should see these hard hats with their gold teeth an' their muscle shirts, wantin' to get rid of a wrapper, a smoke, an old cassette. I know what you're up to guy, I say, I got your number. Could be a crush. A crush o' people. Guess I could wear my zip-up one more day.

Grace looks at her reflection. She turns.

GRACE: Sugar. Thank you. For my birthday present.

SUGAR: You're welcome.

Grace exits. Sugar and Trout are left alone. They kiss.

SUGAR: Truth.

TROUT: Truth.

Sugar faints. Trout catches her. They laugh. Furious love.

Trout's toilet kit.

A last look back, and then into the sun.

On their heels, the sound of a rainstorm.

Epilogue

A year later. Squealing tires. Grace comes in through the front door. Boots and coveralls on. Her hair is tame, unsculpted, no makeup. Thunderstorm.

GRACE: You're home. I'm home. You're home. I'm home. You're home. I'm home Sugar, I'm home.

Grace gets a soda from the fridge. She goes to open it. Decides against it. Puts it back. Thinks about making dinner. Decides against it. She sits on the couch. Stares at the television. Mute. It stares back. She looks at Smith's Recognizable Patterns of Human Malformation *lying on the coffee table. Shock, horror, compassion. She pulls an envelope out of her coverall pocket. She reads.*

GRACE: My sister, my twin,

As promised I am far away.

We have gone north searching for the death place of Mr. Sylvester and Mrs. Mayfair Stanley. I feel sure we will find what we have come looking for.

I am writing this on the night of our thirty-first birthday. This has given me occasion to reflect. Reflect I will.

It appears we broke the death spell. It appears we are free of our particular curse which started in the canal – before we even were. When we were innocent. Now, we can be innocent again.

I know that you kissed Trout to protect me. You suspected him of being a murderer. I can assure you he is not, though, as we both know, he was one once. We still have not been married. I will wait for you to walk that aisle as we done – dotted line – done promised. The big news is: I'm pregnant. An' looks like we're havin' twins. We've already settled on the names. I chose Bird for the bird babies. An' Trout chose Angel 'cause he likes it so much.

The news of the Scrabble Champ Stripper, her murder solved, reached us here in our northern clime. We saw the cameras roll over the shamed face of that teenage hunter, his conscience a homing pigeon, leading him to confess exactly one year to the day of her disappearance. A boy blushing fiery birthmarks. An accident. All accidents are meteors. They change the face of the earth forever.

Grace folds up the letter — knowing it by rote, by rote.

You were right Grace. There is a whole world out here. One that I could never have possibly imagined. I have seen some terrible and beautiful things. Like bein' inside the Holy Mother's fever. Or Madame Button Mushroom Avril's cancer o' the mind. The world is a peculiar place. I have felt afraid.

Sugar appears — lit celestial — above the pines.

SUGAR/GRACE: But mostly I have felt like I am flyin'. Flyin' high above our life, above this planet, this indescribable planet, searchin', wonderin' where to land.
    I love you my sister.

SUGAR: Trout says hello.
    I hope you like your present.
    Happy birthday,
    Your twin,
    Sugar.

Sugar vanishes.

Grace puts the letter away. She sits on the couch. She gets up. Opens the front door. Pulls in a box, perfectly wrapped. She unwraps it. She pulls out a figurine of Sugar. She looks at it for a long time. Sits down on the couch. Turns on the television. Hunting season. A bolt of lightning. Blackout.

Acknowledgements

I am thankful for the passion and intelligence I have encountered along the way, especially: Eda Holmes, Natasha Mytnowych, Michelle Giroux, Melody Johnson, Gord Rand; Ken Gass and the Factory Theatre; Pamela Halstead, Ingrid Rae Doucet, Michael Kash, Krista Laveck and the Ship's Company Theatre; Alana Wilcox; Maureen Labonté, John Murrell, Morwyn Brebner, the actors and actresses who workshopped the play.

Thank you to Jason Logan for unearthing the tablets.

This work was made possible by the support of the Ontario Arts Council's Chalmers Arts Fellowship, the Banff PlayRites Colony and the Canada Council.

Thank you always to Don Kerr, my family and my friends.

About the Author

Plays: *Beaver* (Factory Theatre, Horse Trade Theatre Group in New York, Théâtre La Licorne in Montreal and Presentation House Theatre in Vancouver, published by Playwrights Canada Press), *The Gwendolyn Poems* (Factory Theatre, published by Playwrights Canada Press, Governor General's Award nominee, Trillium Award finalist), *Trout Stanley* (Ship's Company Theatre, Factory Theatre, Dora Award Nominee). Claudia is a graduate of McGill University and the National Theatre School, where she now works as a guest artist. She is currently writing a novella.

Typeset in Centaur and printed and bound at
the Coach House on bpNichol Lane, 2005

Edited by Alana Wilcox
Cover and illustrations by Jason Logan
Author photo by Marni Grossman

Coach House Books
401 Huron Street on bpNichol Lane
Toronto, Ontario
M5S 2G5

416 979 2217 | 800 367 6360

mail@chbooks.com
www.chbooks.com